NANCY TUMINELLY

Cool WHEAT-FREE RECIPES

DELICIOUS & FUN FOODS WITHOUT GLUTEN

A Division of ABDO

ABDO
Publishing Company

visit us at www.abdopublishing.com

Published by ABDO Publishing Company, a division of ABDO, P.O. Box 398166, Minneapolis, Minnesota 55439. Copyright © 2013 by Abdo Consulting Group, Inc. International copyrights reserved in all countries. No part of this book may be reproduced in any form without written permission from the publisher. Checkerboard Library™ is a trademark and logo of ABDO Publishing Company.

Printed in the United States of America, North Mankato, Minnesota
102012
012013

Design and Production: Mighty Media, Inc.
Series Editor: Liz Salzmann
Photo Credits: Aaron DeYoe, Shutterstock

The following manufacturers/names appearing in this book are trademarks: Pyrex®, Kitchen Aid®, Argo®, The Spice Hunter®, 365 Everyday Value™, Ortega®, Tinkyáda®, Contadina™, Lea & Perrins®, Spice Trend®, Betty Crocker®, Nestlé®, Roundy's®, Bob's Red Mill®, Ancient Harvest®, Erawan Brand, Arrowhead Mills®

Library of Congress Cataloging-in-Publication Data

Tuminelly, Nancy, 1952-
  Cool wheat-free recipes : delicious & fun foods without gluten / Nancy Tuminelly.
    pages cm. -- (Cool recipes for your health)
  Audience: 8-12
  Includes bibliographical references and index.
  ISBN 978-1-61783-586-5
  1. Cooking--Juvenile literature. 2. Wheat-free diet--Recipes--Juvenile literature. I. Title.
  TX652.5.T8425 2013
  641.5'6318--dc23
                    2012024003

TO ADULT HELPERS

This is your chance to introduce newcomers to the fun of cooking! As children learn to cook, they develop new skills, gain confidence, and make some delicious food.

These recipes are designed to help children cook fun and healthy dishes. They may need more adult assistance for some recipes than others. Be there to offer help and guidance when needed, but encourage them to do as much as they can on their own. Also encourage them to be creative by using the variations listed or trying their own ideas. Building creativity into the cooking process encourages children to think like real chefs.

Before getting started, establish rules for using the kitchen, cooking tools, and ingredients. It is important for children to have adult supervision when using sharp tools, the oven, or the stove.

Most of all, be there to cheer on your new chefs. Put on your apron and stand by. Watch and learn. Taste their creations. Praise their efforts. Enjoy the culinary adventure!

CONTENTS

WHEAT-FREE

GLUTEN is a chemical found in wheat, barley, and **rye**.
It is the part of wheat that some people are allergic to.
A wheat-free diet is often also called a *gluten-free diet*.

LEARN MORE ABOUT COOKING WHEAT-FREE MEALS!

Following a wheat-free diet means that you don't eat anything made with wheat. This includes many types of bread, cake, pastry, and pasta. Some people don't eat wheat because they don't like the taste. Other people have a condition called **celiac disease**. That means eating wheat makes them feel sick.

There are a lot of foods for people who don't eat wheat. Try some of the wheat-free recipes in this book!

When shopping, look for fresh ingredients. Be sure to avoid things that might be made with wheat. Read the labels carefully.

Sometimes a recipe that includes wheat will list wheat-free **options** for those ingredients. Or, be creative and make up your own **variations**. Being a chef is all about using your imagination.

SAFETY FIRST!

Some recipes call for activities or ingredients that require caution. If you see these symbols, ask an adult for help!

Hot - This recipe requires handling hot objects. Always use oven mitts when holding hot pans.

Sharp - You need to use a sharp knife or cutting tool for this recipe. Ask an adult to help out.

Nuts - This recipe includes nuts. People who are allergic to nuts should not eat it.

THE BASICS

ASK PERMISSION

Before you cook, ask **permission** to use the kitchen, cooking tools, and ingredients. If you'd like to do something yourself, say so! If you would like help, ask for it!

BE NEAT AND CLEAN

- Start with clean hands, clean tools, and a clean work surface.
- Wear comfortable clothing.
- Tie back long hair and roll up your sleeves so they stay out of the food.

NO GERMS ALLOWED!

Raw eggs and raw meat have bacteria in them that can make you sick. After you handle raw eggs or meat, wash your hands, tools, and work surfaces with soap and water. Keep everything clean!

BE PREPARED

- Be organized. Knowing where everything is makes cooking easier!
- Read the directions all the way through before you start cooking.
- Set out all your ingredients before starting.

BE SMART, BE SAFE

- Never work alone in the kitchen.
- Ask an adult before using anything hot or sharp, such as a stove top, oven, knife, or **grater**.
- Turn pot handles toward the back of the stove to avoid accidentally knocking them over.

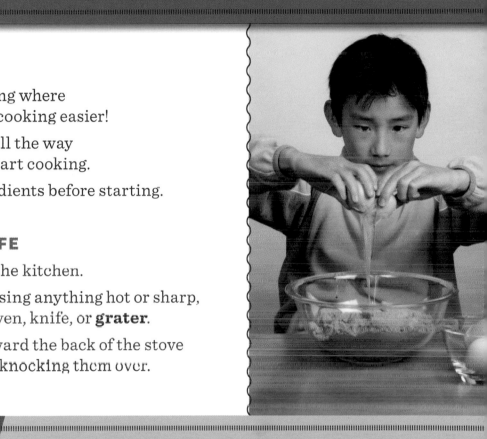

MEASURING

Many ingredients are measured by the cup, tablespoon, or teaspoon. Some ingredients are measured by weight in ounces or pounds. You can buy food by its weight too.

THE TOOL BOX

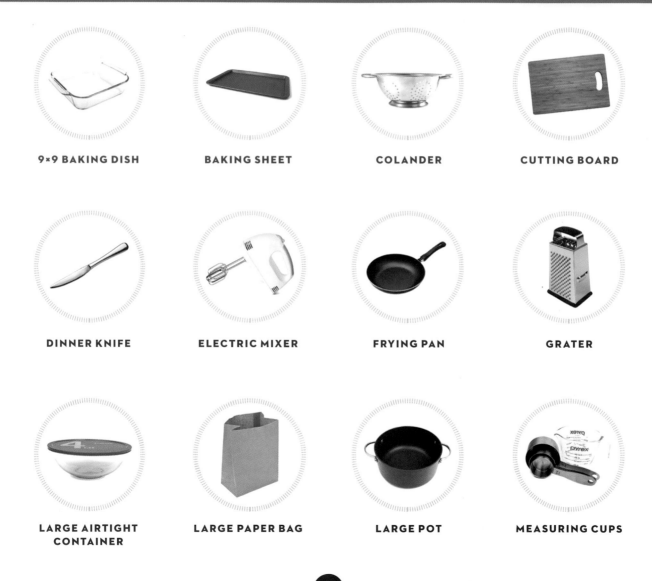

9×9 BAKING DISH

BAKING SHEET

COLANDER

CUTTING BOARD

DINNER KNIFE

ELECTRIC MIXER

FRYING PAN

GRATER

LARGE AIRTIGHT CONTAINER

LARGE PAPER BAG

LARGE POT

MEASURING CUPS

The tools you will need for the recipes in this book are listed below. When a recipe says to use a tool you don't recognize, turn back to these pages to see what it looks like.

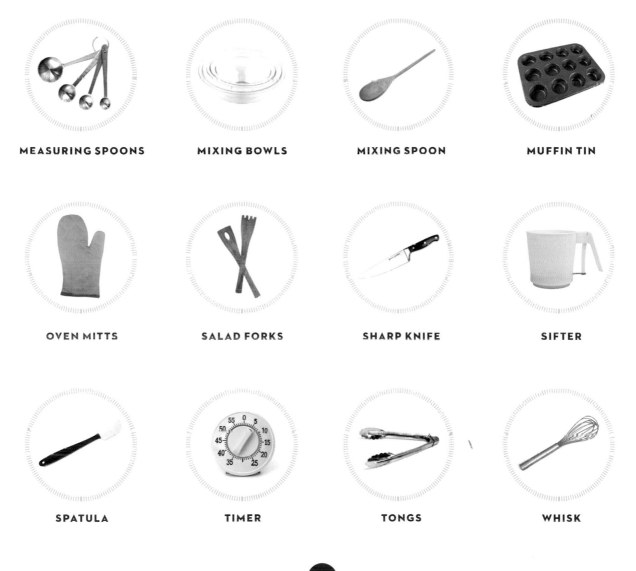

MEASURING SPOONS

MIXING BOWLS

MIXING SPOON

MUFFIN TIN

OVEN MITTS

SALAD FORKS

SHARP KNIFE

SIFTER

SPATULA

TIMER

TONGS

WHISK

COOL INGREDIENTS

ALMONDS

APPLE CIDER VINEGAR

AVOCADO

CLUB SODA

CORNSTARCH

FRUIT (PINEAPPLE, BLUEBERRIES)

GARLIC & GARLIC POWDER

GLUTEN-FREE HARD TACO SHELLS AND TACO SEASONING

GLUTEN-FREE LASAGNA NOODLES

GLUTEN-FREE PIZZA SAUCE

GLUTEN-FREE WORCESTERSHIRE SAUCE

HERBS (BASIL, OREGANO)

GLUTEN-FREE FLOUR

amaranth flour, millet flour, potato starch, quinoa flour, sorghum flour, sweet rice flour, tapioca flour, white rice flour, and xanthan gum.

Many of these recipes call for basic ingredients such as baking powder, baking soda, butter, buttermilk, eggs, ketchup, milk, orange juice, pepper, powdered sugar, salt, sour cream, sugar, and non-stick cooking spray. Here are other ingredients needed for the recipes in this book.

ITALIAN SEASONING

MEAT
(GROUND BEEF, CHICKEN BREASTS)

MUSHROOMS

OIL
(OLIVE & PEANUT)

ONION & ONION SALT

POTATO MIX

RICE SQUARES CEREAL

SPICES
(PAPRIKA, CAYENNE)

SPINACH

TOMATOES

UNSWEETENED COCOA POWDER

VANILLA EXTRACT

CHEESE
colby cheese, goat cheese, mozzarella cheese, parmesan cheese, and ricotta cheese.

COOKING TERMS

CHOP

Chop means to cut into small pieces.

COAT

Coat means to cover something with another ingredient or mixture.

DICE

Dice means to cut something into really small pieces with a knife.

DRAIN

Drain means to remove liquid using a strainer or colander.

GRATE

Grate means to shred something into small pieces using a grater.

Always wash fruit and vegetables well. Rinse them under cold water. Pat them dry with a **towel**. Then they won't slip when you cut them.

SIFT

Sift means to push dry ingredients through a screen using a sifter.

STIR

Stir means to mix ingredients together, usually with a large spoon.

SLICE

Slice means to cut food into pieces of the same thickness.

TOSS

Toss means to turn ingredients over to coat them with seasonings.

WHISK

Whisk means to beat quickly by hand with a whisk or fork.

FLOUR MIXTURE

makes 8 cups

INGREDIENTS

2 cups sorghum flour
2 cups millet flour
1½ cups potato starch
½ cup white rice flour
½ sweet rice flour
½ cup tapioca flour
½ cup amaranth flour
½ quinoa flour

TOOLS

measuring cups & spoons
sifter
large mixing bowl
mixing spoon
large airtight container

1/2
CUP

USE THIS MIXTURE FOR THE RECIPES IN THIS BOOK!

1. Use a sifter to sift all of the ingredients into a large bowl.

2. Stir the ingredients together with a mixing spoon.

3. If you are not using the flour mixture immediately, store it in a large, airtight container. Keep it in the refrigerator.

> **REMINDER**
>
> Make sure your work surfaces, pans, and tools are free of gluten. Always read product labels carefully, even if you've bought the product before.

BLUEBERRY PANCAKES

makes 7 servings

INGREDIENTS

butter

2 eggs

2 tablespoons sugar

2½ cups gluten-free flour mixture (page 14)

2 teaspoons baking powder

½ teaspoon baking soda

¼ teaspoon xanthan gum

¼ teaspoon salt

1¼ cups buttermilk

1 teaspoon vanilla extract

1½ cups fresh blueberries

TOOLS

mixing bowls

measuring cups & spoons

whisk

mixing spoon

frying pan

spatula

1. Soften 4 tablespoons of butter. Put it in a medium bowl. Add the eggs and sugar. Whisk until **fluffy**. Set the bowl aside.

2. Put the gluten-free flour, baking powder, baking soda, xanthan gum, and salt in a separate medium bowl. Stir well. Add the flour mixture to the butter mixture. Stir well.

3. Stir in the buttermilk and vanilla extract. Then add the blueberries. Stir gently.

4. Put 1 tablespoon butter in a frying pan over medium heat. Wait for it to melt. Pour in ⅛ cup of pancake batter.

5. Cook until the bottom of the pancake is golden brown. Flip it over with a spatula. Cook until other side is golden brown.

6. Repeat steps 4 and 5 until the batter is gone. Serve with butter and warm maple syrup.

TERRIFIC

AVOCADO TACOS

makes 6 servings

INGREDIENTS

1 tablespoon olive oil

1 pound lean ground beef

½ cup red onion, finely chopped

2 tablespoons gluten-free taco seasoning

6 gluten-free hard taco shells

2 cups spinach

½ cup avocado, sliced

1 cup mozzarella cheese, grated

TOOLS

measuring cups & spoons

frying pan

grater

mixing spoon

sharp knife

cutting board

baking sheet

oven mitts

timer

1   Preheat the oven to 350 degrees.

2   Heat the olive oil in a frying pan over medium-high heat. Add the ground beef. Cook it until all the pink is gone, stirring occasionally. Add the red onion and cook for 2 more minutes.

3   Turn the heat to low. Add the taco seasoning and 3 tablespoons of water. Cook for 3 minutes. Stir frequently.

4   Arrange the taco shells on a baking sheet. Bake for 5 minutes.

5   Put 2½ tablespoons of ground beef in each taco shell.

6   Top each taco with some of the spinach, avocado slices, and grated cheese.

CLASSIC LASAGNA

makes 8 servings

INGREDIENTS

salt

olive oil

12 gluten-free lasagna noodles

1 cup red onion, chopped

4 garlic cloves, minced

2 pounds lean ground beef

30 ounces gluten-free pizza sauce

2 tablespoons Italian seasoning blend

2 eggs

8 ounces goat cheese

16 ounces ricotta cheese

½ cup freshly grated parmesan cheese

½ cup fresh basil, finely chopped

2 teaspoons oregano

16 ounces grated mozzarella cheese

16 ounces grated colby cheese

TOOLS

measuring cups & spoons

large pot

colander

baking sheet

frying pan

mixing bowls & spoon

sharp knife & cutting board

9×9 baking dish

spatula

grater

oven mitts

timer

1 Preheat the oven to 350 degrees.

2 Cook the noodles. Follow the instructions on the package. Drain the noodles. Put the noodles on the baking sheet. Pour one tablespoon of oil over the noodles.

3 Heat 3 tablespoons of oil in the frying pan over medium-high heat. Add the onion and garlic. Cook for 2 minutes, stirring often. Add the beef and 1 teaspoon salt. Cook the meat until the pink is gone. Stir in the pizza sauce and Italian seasoning. Turn heat to low. Cook 10 minutes, stirring often.

4 Put the eggs, goat cheese, ricotta cheese, parmesan cheese, basil, and oregano in a large bowl. Stir well.

5 Spread 1 cup of meat sauce in the baking dish. Lay four lasagna noodles on top. Spread 1 cup of sauce over the noodles. Spread 1 cup of the cheese mixture over the sauce. Add noodles, sauce, and cheese until the noodles are gone.

6 Spread sauce over the top layer of noodles. Sprinkle the grated cheeses on top. Bake one hour or until the top is golden brown.

SPINACH SALAD

makes 5 servings

INGREDIENTS

SALAD

16 ounces fresh spinach leaves, washed and dried

1 cup red onion, thinly sliced

1 cup chopped tomatoes

1 cup sliced mushrooms

½ teaspoon smoked paprika

DRESSING

1 cup olive oil

¾ cup sugar

⅓ cup ketchup

¼ cup apple cider vinegar

1 teaspoon gluten-free Worcestershire sauce

TOOLS

measuring cups & spoons

mixing bowls

whisk

sharp knife

cutting board

salad forks

1 Put the spinach in a large bowl. Gently tear the spinach leaves into smaller, bite-sized pieces.

2 Add the red onion, tomatoes, and mushrooms. Use salad forks to toss the salad.

3 Put all of the salad dressing ingredients in a mixing bowl. Whisk until smooth.

4 Just before serving, sprinkle paprika over the salad. **Drizzle** the dressing on top. Toss again to coat the salad with the dressing.

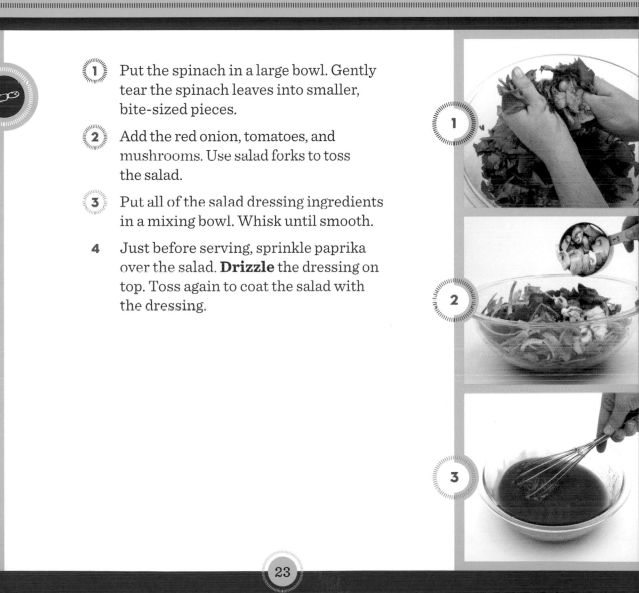

FANTASTIC
CHICKEN FINGERS

makes 6 servings

INGREDIENTS

½ cup cornstarch

1½ cups gluten-free flour mixture (page 14)

1 cup rice squares cereal, crushed

1 teaspoon baking powder

1 teaspoon cayenne powder

1 teaspoon sugar

1 teaspoon garlic powder

1½ teaspoons onion salt

1 teaspoon pepper

12 ounces club soda

1 cup peanut oil

2 pounds boneless, skinless chicken breasts, cut into strips

TOOLS

measuring cups & spoons

clean large paper bag

medium mixing bowl

mixing spoon

large frying pan

tongs

timer

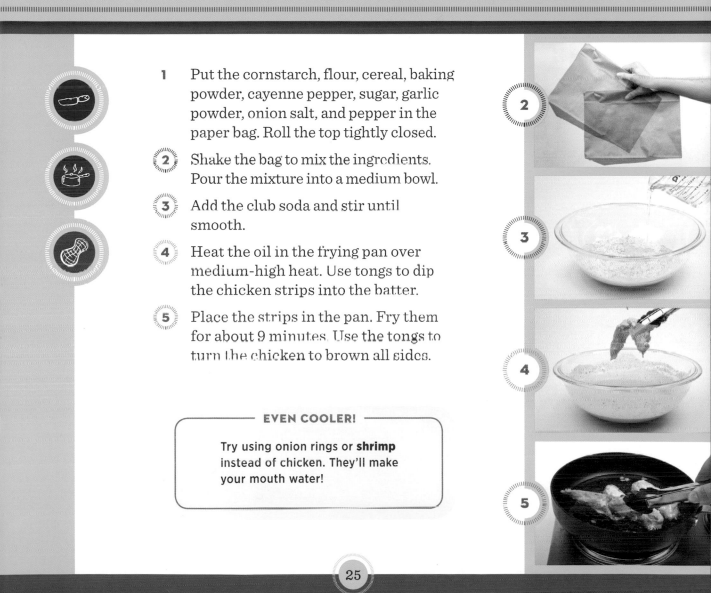

1. Put the cornstarch, flour, cereal, baking powder, cayenne pepper, sugar, garlic powder, onion salt, and pepper in the paper bag. Roll the top tightly closed.

2. Shake the bag to mix the ingredients. Pour the mixture into a medium bowl.

3. Add the club soda and stir until smooth.

4. Heat the oil in the frying pan over medium-high heat. Use tongs to dip the chicken strips into the batter.

5. Place the strips in the pan. Fry them for about 9 minutes. Use the tongs to turn the chicken to brown all sides.

EVEN COOLER!

Try using onion rings or **shrimp** instead of chicken. They'll make your mouth water!

FANCY CUPCAKES

makes 18 cupcakes

INGREDIENTS

CUPCAKES

non-stick cooking spray
1½ cups white rice flour
¾ cup millet flour
½ cup unsweetened cocoa powder
1 teaspoon salt
1 teaspoon baking powder
1 teaspoon baking soda
1 tablespoon xanthan gum
4 eggs
1¼ cups sugar
⅔ cup sour cream
1 cup milk
2 teaspoons vanilla extract

FROSTING

1 cup butter
3½ cups powdered sugar
⅛ teaspoon salt
1 teaspoon milk
2 teaspoons vanilla extract

TOOLS

muffin tin
measuring cups & spoons
mixing bowls
whisk
mixing spoon
oven mitts
electric mixer
dinner knife
timer

1   Preheat the oven to 350 degrees. Coat the muffin tin with cooking spray.

2   Put the rice flour, millet flour, cocoa powder, salt, baking powder, baking soda, and xanthan gum in a medium bowl. Stir well.

3   Put the eggs, sugar, sour cream, milk, and vanilla extract in a separate medium bowl. Whisk until fully blended. Add the flour mixture to the egg mixture. Stir until smooth.

4   Put ¾ cup of batter in each muffin tin cup. Bake for 20 minutes. Set the muffins aside to cool.

5   Make the frosting. Put the butter, powdered sugar, and salt in a medium bowl. Stir well. Add the milk and vanilla extract. Mix with an electric mixer for 4 minutes or until smooth.

6   Spread the frosting on the cupcakes.

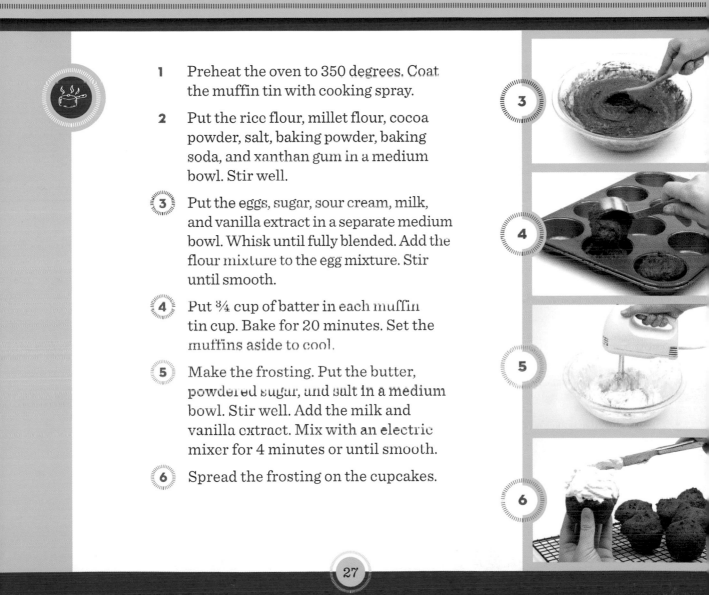

PINEAPPLE MUFFINS

makes 12 muffins

INGREDIENTS

non-stick cooking spray

2 eggs

¾ cup sugar

1 teaspoon vanilla extract

½ cup orange juice

⅓ cup pineapple, diced

⅓ cup almonds, sliced

1½ cups potato mix

½ teaspoon baking powder

TOOLS

muffin tin

measuring cups & spoons

mixing bowls

mixing spoon

sharp knife

cutting board

spatula

oven mitts

timer

1. Preheat the oven to 350 degrees. Coat the muffin tin with cooking spray.

2. Put the eggs, sugar, vanilla extract, and orange juice in a medium bowl. Stir until well blended. The batter should be a little thick. Stir in the pineapple and almonds.

3. Add the potato mix and baking powder. Stir for 30 seconds. Scrape the sides of the bowl with a spatula. This makes sure no flour sticks to the sides or bottom. Stir for 1 minute more.

4. Put the batter in the muffin tin. Each muffin tin cup should be ¾ full.

5. Bake for 18 minutes. Let the muffins cool slightly before serving.

more about WHEAT-FREE LIFE

If you liked these dishes, look for other wheat-free foods. If you want or need to avoid eating wheat, you have a lot of **options**!

Wheat products are often used in cooking and baking. Keep your kitchen stocked with healthy, wheat-free **alternatives** for those ingredients. Some great wheat substitutes to try include corn, rice, potatoes, and buckwheat flour.

Now you're ready to start making your own wheat-free recipes. It takes creativity and planning. Check out different cookbooks. Look through the lists of ingredients. You'll be surprised how many dishes don't need wheat. Or you can come up with your own recipes or **variations**. The kitchen is calling!

Buckwheat isn't a type of wheat at all!
That means it can be part of a wheat-free diet.

GLOSSARY

ALTERNATIVE - something you can choose instead.

CELIAC DISEASE - a condition that affects the small intestine and causes a bad reaction to eating wheat, barley, and rye gluten.

DRIZZLE - to pour in a thin stream.

FLUFFY - light, soft, and airy.

OPTION - something you can choose.

PERMISSION - when a person in charge says it's okay to do something.

RYE - a cereal grass grown for its grain.

SHRIMP - a small shellfish often caught for food.

TOWEL - a cloth or paper used for cleaning or drying.

VARIATION - a change in form, position, or condition.

INDEX

A
adult assistance, 3, 5, 7

B
bacteria, from raw ingredients, 6
bread, recipe for, 28–29
breakfast dish, recipe for, 16–17
buckwheat, 30

C
celiac disease, 5
cheese, types of, 11
chicken snack, recipe for, 24–25
chopping, 12
cleaning, guidelines for, 6
coating, 12
creativity, in cooking, 3, 30
cupcakes, recipe for, 26–27

D
dessert, recipe for, 26–27
dicing, 12
draining, 12

G
gluten-free diet, 4
gluten-free flour
    recipe for, 14–15
    types of, 10
grating, 12

I
ingredients
    basics of, 11
    cleaning of, 6, 13
    freshness of, 5
    measuring of, 7
    preparing of, 7
    types of, 10–11

L
lasagna, recipe for, 20–21

M
main dishes, recipes for, 18–19,
    20–21
measuring, of ingredients, 7
muffins, recipe for, 28–29

P
pancakes, recipe for, 16–17
permission, for kitchen use, 6
preparing, for cooking, 7

R
raw ingredients, bacteria from, 6
rules, for kitchen use, 3

S
safety, guidelines for, 3, 5, 7
salad, recipe for, 22–23
side dish, recipe for, 22–23
sifting, 13
slicing, 13
snack, recipe for, 24–25
stirring, 13

T
tacos, recipe for, 18–19
terms, for cooking methods, 12–13
tools
    cleaning of, 6
    types of, 8–9
tossing, 13

W
web sites, about cooking, 31
wheat-free diet, 5, 30
wheat-free options, 5, 30
whisking, 13